Bikers' Day Out

by A. R. Griffiths

Illustrated by Jolyon Webb

Chapter 1

My name is Leroy King. This is the story of what happened to me and my mates last summer. I still don't understand it. I only know I'll never forget it. My mates, Dave and Spud, feel the same.

The three of us were out for a ride in the country on our bikes. It was warm and sunny, and we had the freedom of long straight empty roads. My bike was soaring like a bird. I was trying out my new leathers. Perfect! But then things changed.

In the afternoon Spud's bike began playing up. First it seemed to lose power when pulling uphill. Later it began spluttering, and finally it died.

We stopped by the roadside and took our helmets off. We saw petrol dripping from Spud's carburettor. I turned off the petrol tap.

Spud groaned. "What a place to break down!"

I looked up and down the road. No signs of life. Just fields all around and a few trees.

Dave noticed a signpost. It said *Ashbury 15 miles*.

"Looks like we're in the middle of nowhere!" he said.

Dave was right. More right than he knew.

Chapter 2

Spud's a new biker and doesn't know much about engines yet. So I said, "Don't worry, mate. It's probably just a bit of dirt under the needle valve."

"And you may have oiled up the plug," said Dave.

Spud looked at me. "Can we fix it?"

I nodded. "Sure, we can fix it. But I've only got a couple of spanners with me. Did anyone bring a screwdriver?"

Spud shook his head.

Dave said, "I only brought some chocolate."

I felt annoyed with myself. I usually carry a load of tools.

"Well, we're stuck without a screwdriver," I said.

Spud began to worry. "What are we going to do? The last town we passed was ten miles back. The next town is fifteen miles on!"

Dave sat down on a rock. He grinned. "I hope you've got your walking boots on, Spud!"

At that moment there was a gust of wind and the sky began to change colour. It was weird. One minute there was a clear blue sky, the next minute everything was grey.

"I reckon it's going to tip down with rain," I said.

Even as I spoke, the first drops of rain fell. This was no ordinary summer shower. Rain came down so hard that the road looked like a bubbling river.

The rain lashed our heads and we put on our helmets fast. There was now a strong wind blowing.

Dave pointed to a big oak tree. "Come on! Let's take shelter!"

Before I had the chance to answer, he was wheeling his bike into the field. Spud and I followed with our bikes.

We stood under the tree and watched the clouds. We could hear the rumble of thunder not far off.

I shouted above the noise of the wind. "We can't stay here. It's too dangerous in a thunder storm!"

Spud tugged at my sleeve. "Look!" He pointed across the field to an old stone house. It had bare windows and looked empty. There was a track leading to it.

"Right! Let's go!" shouted Dave. He led the way with his bike. Spud and I followed.

As we battled through the rain, I thought it was strange that we hadn't seen the house before.

Chapter 3

When we got near the house we saw a stable block. It had a large door swinging on its hinges. We headed straight for it and went in with our bikes.

Inside, we took off our helmets and wet leathers.

"We're lucky to find this place!" said Dave.

Spud brushed a cobweb from his face. "Feels a bit spooky to me," he said.

I looked round. There were about ten stalls. Horse tack was hanging on the walls. "At least we're in the dry," I said.

Just then, I noticed an odd smell. It was like the smell you get at bike races. I peered through the gloom, but it was hard to see much. Then a sudden flash of lightning lit up an arch at the far end of the stable block.

Thunder raged overhead. I went to the door and looked out. There was another lightning flash and for a moment the old stone house was stark silvery white against the grey sky.

Spud sat hunched on a pile of sacks. "I used to hate thunder storms when I was a kid," he said. There was another deafening thunder clap. "I still do!" he added.

I sat down next to Spud and began talking about the last motocross we'd been to. Anything to get his mind off the storm.

Then Dave's voice rang out from half-way along the stable block. "Leroy! Spud! Come and see what I've found!"

As we went towards Dave, I noticed that odd smell again. When we saw what Dave had found, we could hardly believe our eyes.

It was a vintage motorcycle!

Chapter 4

We stood and gazed at the old bike.

"What a beauty! I wonder who owns it," said Dave.

"I thought this place was empty," said Spud.

"It is ... I think," I said.

I bent down to have a closer look at the machine. I reckon it was from the nineteen twenties, but well kept. The petrol tank was under the top tube of the frame, and there were no rear springs. There was a number plate at the front as well as the back.

I moved to the front of the bike. Then I noticed a work bench with tools on it.

I picked up a screwdriver. It was an old one with a wooden handle. "Look! Just what we need!"

Spud looked much happier as he wheeled his bike to the open door of the stables. I needed what little daylight there was.

I set to work on Spud's bike. The screwdriver was just the right size. It didn't take long to find what was wrong. As I thought, there was dirt under the needle valve.

I was about to show Spud what I'd found, when I heard him scream.

I looked up. Spud was standing rigid. He was staring at Dave, who was wearing a horse's nose-bag and blinkers.

"I was only joking, horsing about!" said Dave.

Spud wasn't in the mood for games. He turned and pointed towards the archway at the end of the stables. His hand was shaking. The fear was plain on his face. "I can hear knocking," he said.

"It's your knees knocking," said Dave.

Spud stood rooted to the spot. "Shut up!" he said.

"Spud, look here," I cut in. I showed him what was wrong with his bike.

After I'd finished the job, I looked outside. There was now a thick fog.

Chapter 5

"Spud, I think I've fixed your bike," I said. "Try and start her up."

When the engine sprang into life it was music to our ears. Spud wanted to ride off right away. But I managed to get him to calm down and stop the engine.

I was thinking hard. "I think we'd better stay here for a while," I said.

Spud gave me a look. "WHAT?"

"There's thick fog now," I said. "It's not safe for us to ride in."

Dave agreed with me. "Yes, let's face it. We might have to stay the night."

Spud was about to speak when a bat swooped down. He ducked and almost fell over.

Dave laughed. "You're not scared of a mouse with wings, are you?"

Spud suddenly turned on Dave. "Yes, I am scared!" he shouted. "And I'm not scared to admit it! OK?"

Dave looked first at me, then at Spud. "OK, mate, I'm sorry," he said. Then he took a squashed bar of chocolate from his pocket and offered it to Spud.

While Spud and Dave were eating the chocolate, I got some straw and covered it with sacks.

"Everything will be all right," I said. "There's nothing to worry about."

I sounded braver than I felt. But it worked. Spud sat down on one of the sacks. Then he lay down and curled up in a ball.

Dave just flopped down and yawned out loud.

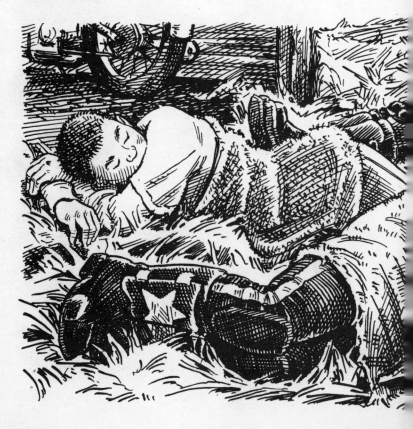

After a while it was quiet everywhere. The storm seemed to have passed over. As my eyes closed I could hear an owl hooting. It was an eerie sound.

Chapter 6

I woke up to hear a voice calling out, "Hey, you three, you're trespassing!"

I sat up and blinked. The light was so strong I could hardly focus on the man. He was a farm worker on a tractor.

"I wouldn't stay here if I were you," he said. "This is where the manor house burnt down years ago. Strange things have happened here. Even I don't hang about!"

With that he drove off.

I rubbed my eyes. Then I turned to see Dave and Spud sitting on the grass behind me. They both looked dazed. Behind them were our bikes with our helmets and leathers.

I walked about a bit. The grass was bone dry and littered with old stones. There was no sign of a house or stables.

Spud spoke first. "What's happened? I thought we went to sleep in some stables."

"I thought that too!" said Dave.

"Yes! We were sheltering from a storm!" I said.

We looked at each other. We all felt puzzled.

Spud said, "I remember we found a bike in the stables!"

"It was an old bike," said Dave.

"A vintage bike," I added.

We talked a bit more and compared notes. We couldn't work it out, no matter how we tried. We could only agree that something very strange had happened.

Spud shuddered. "Let's get away from here!"

We ran to our bikes and pulled on our leathers. That was when I saw something lying in the grass. It was a wooden-handled screwdriver. I picked it up quickly and put it in my pocket. I knew if Spud saw it he'd panic.

We leaped on to our bikes, pulled on our helmets, and made for the road. We headed for home as fast as we could.

What happened that day is still a mystery to us. But it did happen. I've still got the old screwdriver to prove it.